Volume

Contributing Author

Alison S. Marzocchi, Ph.D.

Consultant

Colleen Pollitt, M.A.Ed.
Math Support Teacher
Howard County Public Schools

Publishing Credits

Rachelle Cracchiolo, M.S.Ed., *Publisher*
Conni Medina, M.A.Ed., *Editor in Chief*
Dona Herweck Rice, *Series Developer*
Emily R. Smith, M.A.Ed., *Series Developer*
Diana Kenney, M.A.Ed., NBCT, *Content Director*
Stacy Monsman, M.A., *Editor*
Michelle Jovin, M.A., *Associate Editor*
Fabiola Sepulveda, *Graphic Designer*

Image Credits: p.16 Juniors Bildarchiv GmbH/Alamy; p.19 (top) Thomas Frey/dpa/picture-alliance/Newscom; p.24 Design Pics / Corey Hochachka/Corey Hochachka/Newscom; p.25 Chris Mattison/Minden; p.27 Marc Romanelli/Blend Images/Newscom; all other images from iStock and/or Shutterstock.

Library of Congress Cataloging-in-Publication Data

Names: Stark, Kristy, author.
Title: Terrarium pets / Kristy Stark, M.A.Ed.
Description: Huntington Beach, CA : Teacher Created Materials, [2019] |
   Series: Amazing animals | Audience: Grade 4 to 6. | Includes index. |
   Identifiers: LCCN 2018051879 (print) | LCCN 2018052962 (ebook) | ISBN
   9781425855352 (eBook) | ISBN 9781425858919 (paperback)
Subjects: LCSH: Reptiles as pets--Juvenile literature. | Spiders as
   pets--Juvenile literature. | Scorpions as pets--Juvenile literature. |
   Amphibians as pets--Juvenile literature. | Terrariums--Juvenile literature.
Classification: LCC SF459.R4 (ebook) | LCC SF459.R4 S725 2019 (print) | DDC
   639.3/9--dc23
LC record available at https://lccn.loc.gov/2018051879

Teacher Created Materials

5301 Oceanus Drive
Huntington Beach, CA 92649-1030
www.tcmpub.com

ISBN 978-1-4258-5891-9
© 2019 Teacher Created Materials, Inc.
Printed in Malaysia
Thumbprints.21254

Table of Contents

The Perfect Home for Unusual Pets

When people think about pets, they usually think of dogs, cats, or birds. These animals make great pets, of course, but not all pets have fur or feathers. Animals with scales, gills, or eight legs can make ideal pets too. Snakes and geckos can be pets. So can salamanders and tarantulas. However, most pet owners do not want these types of pets roaming freely around their homes.

That is where **terrariums** come in. These enclosures are like aquariums for pet fish, but they are made for **terrestrial** animals. Terrariums come in many shapes and sizes. Sometimes, they are used to grow plants. But they are also used to keep pets, such as bugs, reptiles, and amphibians. Pet owners place exactly what these animals need inside the terrariums. They can **tailor** the terrarium's habitat to the specific requirements of the pet they choose to keep. For example, a terrarium can reflect a desert habitat for a pet snake. Or it can contain a wet habitat for pet frogs.

Regardless of the type of pet or habitat, terrariums allow pet owners to watch their pets without the worry of the critters escaping from their homes.

A boy places his royal python in a desert-themed habitat.

LET'S EXPLORE MATH

Brothers Brad and Louie want to buy a new pet frog. They have a small terrarium they once used for a hermit crab. They want to determine its volume to see if it is large enough for a frog. They both use 1-inch cubes but have different strategies. Use the pictures of their strategies to answer the questions.

1. How are the strategies similar? How are they different?

2. Which strategy would you use and why?

3. Do you think this tank is the right size for a pet frog? Why or why not?

Brad's Strategy

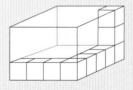

Louie's Strategy

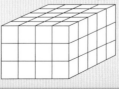

Raising Reptiles

People who want a different type of pet than everyone else might consider reptiles. Many types of reptiles make good pets. They **thrive** in the environment that pet owners create inside terrariums.

Bearded Dragon

In the wild, bearded dragons are only found in Australia. But people don't have to live Down Under to see one. Bearded dragons are a very popular type of lizard to keep as a pet because they like to be around people. They are also easy to care for and feed.

Male bearded dragons grow to be 12–24 inches (30–61 centimeters) long from their head to the tip of their tail. Females are typically smaller than males. Usually, a terrarium that is about 48 × 18 × 21 in. (122 × 46 × 53 cm) is big enough for a single bearded dragon. A larger tank may be needed for a bearded dragon over 20 in. (51 cm) long.

Since they are **native** to Australia, bearded dragons are used to a hot and dry environment. Even as pets, they need a home that is hot and dry. Terrarium lights replicate their natural habitat. The lights provide heat that **mimics** the sun. Their home should also have a log or branch for climbing. Bearded dragons like to hide, so including a cardboard box or other hiding place is an easy way to keep them entertained.

A bearded dragon tries to catch a grasshopper.

LET'S EXPLORE MATH

A typical bearded dragon terrarium has dimensions of 48 × 18 × 21 inches.

1. Sketch the terrarium. Label length, width, and height.

2. Find the volume of the tank.

Typically, bearded dragons need surface temperatures from 95 to 110 degrees Fahrenheit (35 to 43.3 degrees Celsius). All reptiles are **cold-blooded**, so they need heat from the sun or lights to warm their bodies. They cannot maintain a **consistent** body temperature on their own like warm-blooded animals, such as humans, dogs, and cats, can. Therefore, reptiles spend large portions of the day **basking** in the sun or light to warm themselves.

When they are not warming themselves, bearded dragons are fun pets to watch. They get their name from the "beards" on the bottom of their throats. They often puff out their beards, wave their arms, and bob their heads up and down. It is also fun to watch them hunt for crickets and worms that owners place in their tanks. They are even able to perch on a person's shoulder!

Bearded dragons can live 10–15 years in captivity. Their tame and friendly behavior makes bearded dragons a fun choice for a pet.

Corn Snake

Another good choice for a first-time reptile owner is a pet corn snake. These snakes are not **venomous**, so they are not dangerous. In fact, corn snakes are very calm. There are many different species of corn snakes. Depending on the species, they range in color from reddish-brown to white with colorful spots or bands.

A corn snake wraps around a branch in a terrarium.

Ideally, the terrarium for a corn snake should be at least as long as the snake to give the pet plenty of room to move around. However, an adult snake can grow to be 3–6 feet (1–1.8 meters) long. Many snake owners have to get smaller enclosures. The absolute smallest it should be is 30 × 12 × 12 in. (76 × 30 × 30 cm). Owners should put a box inside the terrarium because snakes like privacy. A corn snake will go inside the box to escape watchful eyes. Snakes also like to climb, so owners should include branches or posts that they can slither up. A pan of water will make the terrarium a bit **humid**. Make sure to have a secure wire mesh lid on the terrarium because corn snakes are very good at escaping through small openings.

LET'S EXPLORE MATH

Leslie buys a 30 × 12 × 12 inch terrarium for her corn snake. She finds the volume by performing these calculations:

$30 \times 12 = 360$

$360 + 360 + 360 + 360 + 360 + 360 + 360 + 360 + 360 + 360 + 360 + 360 = 4{,}320$

1. Describe what Leslie is thinking. Is her strategy correct? Why or why not?

2. Is Leslie's strategy the most efficient way to solve the problem? Why or why not?

Like all snakes, corn snakes periodically shed their skin as they outgrow it. The humidity inside the terrarium helps them shed, and the process happens over the course of a few weeks. It is interesting to watch, but experts say to avoid handling a snake while it is shedding. Its new skin is fragile and can tear.

Feeding corn snakes is also interesting. They eat a mouse or rat every few days. Owners can buy frozen mice and rats at pet stores and online. The meal must first be defrosted before it can be served. It is fascinating to observe corn snakes swallow their meal whole!

Corn snakes are easy to care for and can live from 15 to 20 years. They require little maintenance and don't mind being handled, which makes them an ideal pet for some people.

A corn snake sheds its skin.

A corn snake eats a mouse.

...opard geckos are great reptiles for beginners to own. They are
...small and can easily be handled by their owners. They are usually
...t 8–10 in. (20–25 cm) long from head to tail.

...opard geckos thrive in terrariums. Geckos live 6–10 years, but some
...s can live 20 years or more as pets. A single leopard gecko needs a
...enclosure that measures 24 × 12 × 12 in. (61 × 30 × 30 cm). Owners
...d provide hiding and climbing spaces in the terrarium. These may
...e half logs or small cardboard boxes. The bottom of the tank can
...ed with paper, carpet, mulch, or small rocks. However, owners
...l avoid wood chips because the wood pieces can cut the geckos'
...feet.

...e other reptiles, geckos bask in the heat during the day. Their
...should include a regular light bulb to provide heat for basking.
...d 88°F (31°C) is a good temperature for basking during the day.

...terrarium should also include a shallow dish of water. The gecko
...nk from this dish, as well as soak itself. The dish also provides a
...umidity, which aids the shedding of their skin when needed.

...ard geckos eat mostly crickets and worms. Young geckos are fed
...hile adults only need to eat every few days.

A leopard gecko soaks
in a dish of water.

A leopard gecko pulls off its shedding skin.

Eight-Legged Pets

Some people don't cringe or squeal when spiders or scorpions are mentioned. They keep them as pets! But they can't make any eight-legged creature they find their pet. Experts recommend only certain kinds of spiders and scorpions be kept in homes. These creatures have been bred and raised to be pets, so they are safe to keep.

Potential owners should also be aware that some species of spiders and scorpions are endangered because too many have been taken from the wild to be sold as pets. Plus, many species in the wild have suffered major loss of their natural habitats.

Spiders and scorpions are in a class of creatures called *arachnids*. They share common features, such as two body sections and four pairs of legs.

emperor scorpion

Pinktoe Tarantula

There are many different spider species that can make good pets. The pinktoe tarantula is a popular choice because of its calm **temperament**. The pinktoe gets its name from the pink coloring at the end of each of its legs.

Pinktoes are tree-dwelling tarantulas, so taller terrariums work best. They have a leg span of about 3.5–5 in. (about 9–13 cm). Many owners turn a 20 × 10 × 12 in. (51 × 25 × 30 cm) enclosure on its side and add a log for the pinktoe to climb. The open side must have a secure lid to prevent the pinktoe from climbing out. It is a good idea to have only one pinktoe in a terrarium of this size because if there are two or more in the same space, the spiders will often try to eat each other.

pinktoe tarantula

Pinktoe tarantulas like a hot and damp environment that is similar to the rain forests in their native homes in Brazil and Costa Rica. The terrarium's temperature should be kept between 78 and 82°F (26 and 28°C). Owners can use lights and heaters to keep the temperature warm enough, especially if they live in a cold place. The humidity level must be 65–75 percent. The humidity can be maintained by placing a bowl of water or a water-soaked sponge in the tank.

Pinktoes are quite calm, but they are fast. Owners should sit on the ground when holding their pinktoes. Pinktoes can be injured when jumping from a high place. Most of the time, they can stay in their terrariums. The terrarium floor needs 2–3 in. (5.1–7.6 cm) of moss or soil. This material provides bedding for the jumping tarantula.

Pinktoe tarantulas enjoy eating. Their diet consists of different types of insects. They can be fed large crickets or grasshoppers. They especially like to capture flying insects, moths being their favorite.

These tarantulas are quiet and take up little space. However, they may not be the best choice for small children since it takes some time for them to get used to being handled.

A man cleans his tarantula terrarium.

pinktoe tarantula

Patricia buys her pinktoe tarantula a terrarium that is 30 centimeters long, 25 centimeters wide, and 51 centimeters tall. She wants to place a layer of soil that is $7\frac{1}{2}$ centimeters deep on the bottom of the terrarium.

1. What is the volume of the soil she needs to purchase?

2. What is the volume of the space in the terrarium not filled with soil?

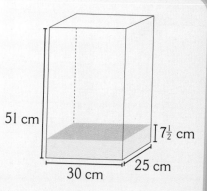

51 cm

$7\frac{1}{2}$ cm

30 cm

25 cm

Emperor Scorpion

Some pet owners choose emperor scorpions for their terrariums. This is partly because emperor scorpions are fairly calm and do not often sting. However, when they do sting, it is similar to a bee sting. In contrast, the stings of other types of scorpions can be much more painful and even deadly.

Most emperor scorpions grow to be about 5–8 in. (13–20 cm) long. They are typically black with green or brown coloring. Their claws, called *pedipalps* (PEH-dih-palps), are quite large and look intimidating.

Emperor scorpions eat crickets and other small insects. Adults are fed one or two crickets every other night. They eat at night because they are **nocturnal**.

These scorpions are native to Africa, where it is warm and damp. So, a humid woodland terrarium is best. Experts recommend using several inches of soil to cover the bottom of the terrarium because scorpions like to **burrow**. Then, cover the soil with moss and leaves. The moss should be kept slightly damp to keep the humidity high in the terrarium. Every day, owners should spray a light mist into the enclosure. Owners should keep a shallow water dish in the terrarium too.

The terrarium's temperature should be regulated to be around 70–90°F (21–32°C). The terrarium should also include places for the scorpion to hide, such as bark, broken flowerpots, or flat stones.

Emperor scorpions can live long lives in captivity, about six to eight years. They are easy to care for. But they can get stressed when handled, so owners should use caution.

emperor scorpion

This scorpion's terrarium has soil, leaves, and pieces of cork in it.

An emperor scorpion eats an insect.

Caring for Amphibians

Amphibians include frogs, toads, salamanders, and newts. Like reptiles and arachnids, there are some amphibian species that make good pets. Many pet owners find that these pets are interesting to watch and care for.

People who consider getting an amphibian for a pet need to know that these creatures should rarely be handled. These pets are mostly for watching. This is because many amphibians' skin has **toxins** that can irritate human skin. If owners need to handle an amphibian, they should always wear gloves.

Buresch's crested newt

Dumpy Tree Frog

Experts say that the dumpy tree frog is a good choice for first-time amphibian owners. There are many varieties of dumpy tree frogs, but the white dumpy tree frogs tend to live the longest. With the perfect conditions, dumpy tree frogs can live up to 20 years. Most will live 7–10 years in captivity. These nocturnal creatures have bright-green skin with white spots on their bellies.

Dumpy tree frogs do not require much care, which makes them a good choice for a pet. Also, they are fairly quiet, so owners do not have to worry about loud croaking during the night.

dumpy tree frog

It is interesting to watch the dumpy tree frog change as it goes through **metamorphosis**. Through this process, it grows from an egg, to a tadpole, to a froglet, to an adult frog. Some pet owners keep a male and a female frog so they can observe this process.

Dumpy tree frogs grow to be 3–5 in. (8–13 cm), with females usually growing a little longer than males. Two adult dumpy tree frogs need a 20 × 10 × 12 in. (51 × 25 × 30 cm) enclosure. The terrarium's temperature should be kept between 68 and 85°F (20 and 29°C), and it must be humid. Owners usually keep it moist by spraying a light mist into the terrarium about twice per week.

Green plants in the tank provide places for the frogs to hide during the day. These frogs have large toe pads that make them good climbers, so owners may want to include branches that allow for climbing.

Once the terrarium is assembled, these frogs do not require much care. They need food, such as small insects and crickets, and fresh water. Owners typically buy live insects from pet stores to feed to their tree frogs.

Like all amphibians, dumpy tree frogs should not be handled often. Instead, owners can sit back and watch their amazing pets climb, eat, and hide in their terrarium homes!

A dumpy tree frog climbs a branch.

Frog Life Cycle

adult frog

froglet

eggs

late tadpole stage

early tadpole stage

LET'S EXPLORE MATH

Vixia builds a custom terrarium for her two dumpy tree frogs. The dimensions are $20 \times 10\frac{3}{4} \times 12\frac{1}{2}$ inches. However, the frogs are growing quickly, and she wants to build a new terrarium with double the volume. Vixia decides that a terrarium with dimensions $40 \times 21\frac{1}{2} \times 25$ inches will have double the volume of the original.

1. Is Vixia's solution correct? Why or why not?

2. Recommend dimensions of a new terrarium that will have triple the volume of the original terrarium. Use words, numbers, or pictures to prove that your solution works.

23

Tiger Salamander

Tiger salamanders are another popular amphibian pet. They are named for the distinct yellow spots or stripes on their black skin. Tiger salamanders are popular pets because they are tame and live for a long time. Some have even lived as long as 25 years! They are also one of the largest salamanders, growing to be 9–10 in. (23–25 cm) as an adult.

A tiger salamander during the **larval** stage needs an aquatic terrarium measuring 24 × 12 × 12 in. (60 × 30 × 30 cm). About 6 in. (15 cm) of water is needed in the tank. A water filter is required to keep the water clean. When the salamander reaches adulthood, the amount of water can be reduced.

In addition to water, salamanders need some dry land. This area is created with a hill of soil or bark chips that slope down into the water. Like many terrarium pets, salamanders like to hide. Their homes should include plants, rocks, or bark that can serve as hiding places.

Room temperature is typically **adequate** for tiger salamanders. So there is no need for additional lights or heating lamps.

Tiger salamanders are **voracious** eaters and can become obese. Salamanders usually dine on crickets and earthworms. As a treat, owners can also feed them a pinkie mouse, which is a young, small mouse that does not yet have fur.

Due to their sensitive skin, tiger salamanders should not be handled often. Pet owners should observe and appreciate these pets without harming them.

A tiger salamander eats a worm.

Miko's tiger salamander terrarium has a water section and a soil section. Which section has a greater volume? Use words, numbers, or pictures to show your thinking.

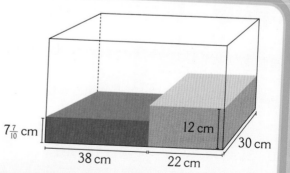

$7\frac{7}{10}$ cm

12 cm

30 cm

38 cm

22 cm

Choosing the Best Pet

There are many pets that will thrive in a terrarium setting—from frogs and lizards to snakes and spiders. The tricky part may be choosing the best one for you! There are many things to consider before potential pet owners make a commitment.

They have to think about how much it will cost to properly care for the pet. Besides the cost for the pet, the costs of the terrarium and its contents must be factored into the equation. Of course, it also costs money to feed the pet.

Pet owners have to think about which pet will be a good fit for their family. It is best to pick a pet that everyone will enjoy. For example, a pinktoe tarantula may not be the best choice if a family member is scared of spiders.

Consider the amount of space a pet will need. If owners only have space for a small terrarium, then they need to choose a small pet, such as a tarantula or scorpion.

When in doubt about which pet to choose, it's always a good idea to ask an expert at a pet store that sells terrarium animals. Also, read books about the pets you are considering, or ask someone you know who has a terrarium pet. Pet owners need to make sure they do their research before making a decision.

Once people finally choose pets, they can enjoy setting up their terrariums. Then it's time to have fun watching and interacting with their new friend!

A woman shops for a terrarium.

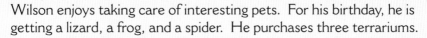
Wilson enjoys taking care of interesting pets. For his birthday, he is getting a lizard, a frog, and a spider. He purchases three terrariums.

- Terrarium A: $18 \times 18 \times 10\frac{3}{10}$ inches
- Terrarium B: $46\frac{1}{2} \times 18 \times 20\frac{1}{2}$ inches
- Terrarium C: $20\frac{1}{2} \times 16\frac{1}{5} \times 10$ inches

Wilson wants to give the largest terrarium to the lizard because it is the largest pet. The smallest terrarium is for the smallest pet, the spider. Which terrarium should he give to each pet? Use words, numbers, or pictures to show your thinking.

A pet expert plays with terrarium animals.

🔩 Problem Solving

Giyong's parents give him permission to keep a terrarium pet. But before they buy the pet, Giyong has to convince them that he has a plan to set up a healthy terrarium appropriate for the pet he chooses.

Giyong's mom gives him an empty $21 \times 18 \times 12$ inch terrarium. His dad gives him these materials:

- $222\frac{1}{2}$ cubic inches of soil

- $146\frac{3}{4}$ cubic inches of wood chips

- 122 cubic inches of water

- sticks filling a $12 \times 14 \times 13$ inch box

- rocks filling a $10\frac{1}{2} \times 10\frac{1}{2} \times 4$ inch box

- leaves filling a $18 \times 8\frac{1}{4} \times 10$ inch box

Use the diagram of the terrarium and the information about the materials to solve the problems and help Giyong with his plan.

1. Will all the materials fit in the terrarium? How do you know?

2. Design a layout for the terrarium. You do not need to use the entire amount of any of the materials, and you do not need to include each item. Label the dimensions of the materials you include.

3. Be sure to leave enough empty space at the top of the terrarium for the pet to move around! What is the volume of the empty space in your terrarium's design?

4. What type of pet do you recommend Giyong choose to live in the terrarium you designed? Why?

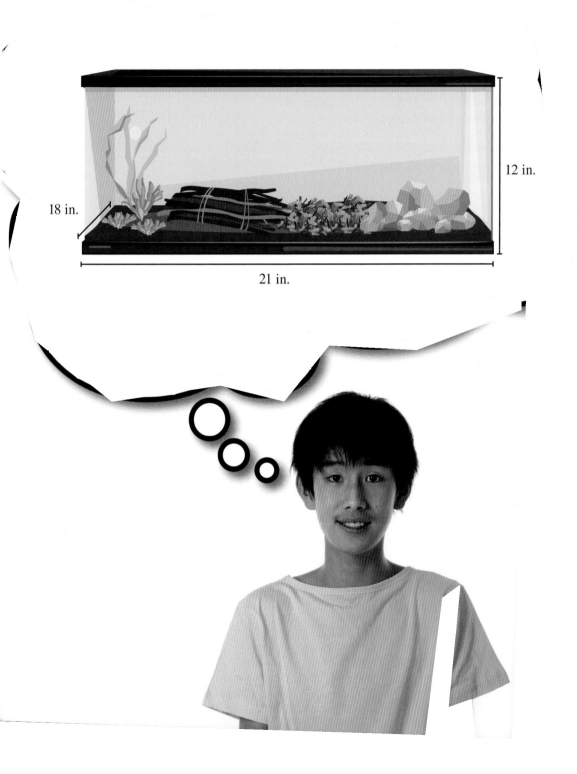

Glossary

adequate—good or acceptable

basking—sitting or relaxing in a bright and warm place

burrow—to make a hole in the ground by digging

cold-blooded—having a body temperature that is similar to the temperature of the environment

consistent—steady or constant

humid—having a lot of moisture in the air

larval—the part of an insect's life where it is in a very young form and looks like a worm

metamorphosis—a major change in the form of some animals or insects that happens as they become adults

mimics—creates the appearance or effect of something

native—produced, living, or existing naturally in a particular region

nocturnal—awake at night and asleep during the day

tailor—to make something fit a specific need

temperament—the normal mood or behavior of an animal or person

terrariums—glass or plastic boxes used for growing plants or keeping small animals indoors

terrestrial—relating to land on Earth

thrive—to grow or develop successfully

toxins—poisonous substances produced by living things

venomous—capable of putting venom into another animal's body by biting or stinging it

voracious—having a large appetite

Index

Answer Key

Let's Explore Math

page 5

1. Both strategies find volume based on the number of unit cubes that fit in the terrarium. Louie counts out all the unit cubes, while Brad only counts cubes forming the length, width, and height. Brad would need to multiply those dimensions to calculate the volume.

2. Answers should include a chosen strategy and reasoning.

3. Answers will vary. Example: *This hermit crab terrarium is probably too small for a frog that is larger than a hermit crab.*

page 7

1. Sketches will vary. Example:

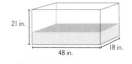

2. 18,144 cu. in.

page 10

1. She finds the area of the base and then the sum of 12 layers. Yes, her strategy is correct because the terrarium has a base area of 360 sq. in. and a height of 12 in.

2. Answers will vary. Example: *Her strategy works, but is not the most efficient. She could multiply the height and base area to calculate the volume.*

page 17

1. 5,625 cm^3

2. 32,625 cm^3

page 23

1. No, its volume is 8 times the original's volume.

2. Answers will vary.
   Examples: $60 \times 10\frac{3}{4} \times 12\frac{1}{2}$ in.;
   $20 \times 32\frac{1}{4} \times 12\frac{1}{2}$ in.; and
   $20 \times 10\frac{3}{4} \times 37\frac{1}{2}$ in.

page 25

water; The water section's volume is 8,778 cm^3 and the soil section's volume is 7,920 cm^3.

page 27

Terrarium A: frog; Terrarium B: lizard; Terrarium C: spider

Problem Solving

1. No; The volume of the terrarium is 4,536 cu. in., but the total volume of the materials is 4,601.25 cu. in.

2. Designs should include a sketch with labeled dimensions.

3. Answers should be the difference between the volume of the empty terrarium and the total volume of materials.

4. Answers should include a chosen pet and explanation of how the terrarium is appropriate.